The

Heart

of

God

The **Heart** of **God**

Woodrow Kroll

President & Bible Teacher
BACK TO THE BIBLE

The quoted ideas expressed in this book (but not scripture verses) are not, in all cases, exact quotations, as some have been edited for clarity and brevity. In all cases, the author has attempted to maintain the speaker's original intent. In some cases, quoted material for this book was obtained from secondary sources, primarily print media. While every effort was made to ensure the accuracy of these sources, the accuracy cannot be guaranteed.

For additions, deletions, corrections, or clarifications in future editions of this text, please contact Paul Shepherd, Executive Director for Elm Hill Books. Email pshepherd@elmhillbooks.com.

Scripture quotations are taken from:

The Holy Bible, King James Version (KJV)

The Holy Bible, New King James Version (NKJV) Copyright © 1982 by Thomas Nelson, Inc. Used by permission.

The Holy Bible, New International Version (NIV) Copyright © 1973, 1978, 1984, by International Bible Society. Used by permission of Zondervan Publishing House. All rights reserved.

Cover Design by Mark Ross
Page Layout by Bart Dawson

ISBN 1-4041-8506-2

Printed in the United States of America

Table of Contents

Introduction

*I*n the movie *The Passion of the Christ,* the crucifixion scene is brought to a close by a large teardrop that splashes down from heaven. The teardrop is a prelude to a violent storm and earthquake that drives all but Jesus' most committed disciples from the foot of the cross. While fictional, the teardrop is a dramatic reminder that God has a heart—a heart broken by man's sin.

As we study the Bible, we find a multitude of references, either directly or indirectly, that reveal God's heart. This text examines the heart of God through 31 devotional readings. Each brief chapter contains Bible verses, a short essay, quotations from noted Christian thinkers, and a prayer. Each chapter is a powerful reminder that God's heart reflects His character. If we want to know God better, we need to know His heart.

Your Heavenly Father loves you in ways that you cannot fully understand. God's heart is filled with care, concern, compassion, empathy, and love. As you read these pages, carefully consider what God's love means to you. And remember: if you genuinely trust your Heavenly Father, and if you allow His Son to reign over your life, you will be held close to God's heart—today, tomorrow, and forever.

1

The Caring Heart of God

Casting all your care upon Him,
for He cares for you.
1 Peter 5:7 NKJV

*D*o you ever have those days when you wonder if anyone cares for you? You can be certain that the heart of God cares for you. God's heart is tender and loving. God cares for us when no one else seems to be concerned. When you and I offer our fears, worries and anxieties to God, we give Him the opportunity to demonstrate how marvelously caring His heart really is, and we allow God to show us how deeply He cares for us.

Peter tells us to "cast" all our cares. This word carries with it the idea of deliberately depositing a burden upon someone or something else. If we were to do that to another person, that person might feel like we were imposing. But it is not so with God. Peter tells us to actually cast it or throw it upon God who will never feel imposed upon, because He cares for us.

Have you humbly opened your heart to Him? Have you taken your worries to Him? Have you accepted the outpouring of love that flows from God's heart? If not, then today is the perfect time to do so. When you do, you will experience a relief like a heavy load has been lifted from your shoulders. And it has, because the heart of God cares for you.

If you wish to leave much wealth to your children,
leave them in God's care.

John Chrysostom

[God] cares about, not just spiritual things like
salvation, justification, sanctification,
and glorification, but also about everyday,
practical things.

Anne Graham Lotz

Cast your cares on God; that anchor holds.

Alfred Lord Tennyson

Praise the Father for His loving kindness;
tenderly cares He for His erring children.
Praise Him.

Elizabeth R. Charles

There's not much you can't achieve or endure if you know God is walking by your side. Just remember: Someone knows, and Someone cares.

–

Bill Hybels

A Prayer

God, Your loving care for me is deeper than I can imagine. Thank You for caring about me when no one else seems to. I will open my heart to You, and I will return Your love today, tomorrow, and throughout eternity.
Amen

2

The Lamenting Heart of God

Jesus wept.
John 11:35 NKJV

*W*hen Christ stood outside the tomb of Lazarus, the brother of Martha and Mary, He was overcome with grief, and He wept. Even though Jesus knew that He was going to raise His friend from the dead, the realization of how sin had caused such misery and suffering, ending in death, ripped His heart apart.

Jesus' response to the death of Lazarus gives us insight into the heart of God: God's heart is a lamenting heart. It feels our pain. When we experience the pangs of human suffering, God suffers with us. When we grieve at the loss of our loved ones, God understands our sadness. He feels it as well, and He stands ready to comfort us whenever we sincerely turn to Him.

Are you sorrowing today? Know that God feels that sorrow too. Give that grief to the One who knows your pain. Then, in His own perfect time and in His own perfect way, He will heal our pain *if* we invite Him to rule over our hearts, our lives, and our souls.

Sometimes love really hurts. It broke the heart of
God to demonstrate His love to us through Christ
but its ultimate end was salvation.

Beth Moore

Let my heart be broken by the things
that break the heart of God.

Bob Pierce

One of the main missions of God is to free us from
the debilitating bonds of fear and anxiety.
God's heart is broken when He sees us
so demoralized and weighed down by fear.

Bill Hybels

When you have nothing left but God,
then you become aware that God is enough.

Maude Royden

God is not a power or principle or law, but he is a living, creating, communicating person—a mind who thinks, a heart who feels, a will who acts, whose best name is Father.

—

Robert Hamill

A Prayer

Lord, it is sometimes more than I can comprehend that You would be willing to connect Your heart to mine in such a way that You feel all that I feel. Your willingness to share in my sorrow and grief makes me love You more than ever before. May I praise Your holy name forever. Amen

3

The Just Heart of God

For the LORD is a God of justice;
blessed are all those
who wait for Him.
Isaiah 30:18 NKJV

*H*ave you ever been in a position where something happened to you that was unjust? Have you ever been unjustly criticized or wrongly accused? And then, have you wondered what you should do about it? Sometimes, the best thing you can do is to turn matters over to God. Why? Because the heart of God is just—and God always makes things right in due time.

There has never been a time when God was not a just God. Moses said it this way to the people of Israel, "Ascribe greatness to our God. He is the Rock, His work is perfect; for all His ways are justice, a God of truth and without injustice; righteous and upright is He" (Deuteronomy 32:3, 4 NKJV).

Moses was convinced that God was a God of justice, and we, too, must be convinced of that fact, even if we might not always see that justice at work. Sometimes you get cheated. Sometimes things happen in your life that you can't understand. Sometimes you say, "God, aren't you watching what they're doing to me?" Sometimes you're just baffled and you become impatient for God to act. If so, be patient. Remember that God's timing is not our timing.

If we had our way, we would balance the books of justice much sooner than it sometimes seems that He does. But we should probably be more cautious in our calls for God's justice. None of us would fair very well if He were to immediately enforce justice for every instance of sin or evil.

Make no mistake about it, though. God's heart is set on justice. The books will balance. We can depend on Him to set all things in order.

To serve God is nothing other than maintaining and preserving justice by good works.

Lactantius

God's compassion flows out of his goodness, and goodness without justice is not goodness. God spares us because he is good, but he could not be good if he were not just.

A. W. Tozer

Man is unjust, but God is just,
and finally justice triumphs.
–

Henry Wadsworth Longfellow

A Prayer

Dear Father of justice, help me to wait patiently for Your plans to unfold. And, when there is injustice in this world, when there are people who are oppressed and in need, use me as an agent of change. May Your justice reign in my life and Your world, now and forever.
Amen

4

The Faithful Heart of God

*Through the Lord's mercies
we are not consumed,
because His compassions fail not.
They are new every morning;
Great is Your faithfulness.*
Lamentations 3:22, 23 NKJV

*T*he Bible makes it perfectly clear that the heart of God is always faithful. The faithfulness of God does not mean we, His children, are freed from life's problems and tragedies. It means that God will preserve us in our difficulties, not from our difficulties.

God's faithfulness is made clear in the beautiful words of Psalm 23:4: "Yea, though I walk through the valley of the shadow of death, I will fear no evil: for thou art with me; thy rod and thy staff they comfort me" (KJV). God does not exempt us from the valleys of life, but neither does He ask us to walk alone. He is always there.

God's heart is faithful to His people; He is faithful to His Word; and He is faithful to you. Paul writes in 1 Corinthians 1:9, "God is faithful, by whom you were called into the fellowship of His Son, Jesus Christ our Lord" (NKJV). God has a faithful heart. Trust Him, and take comfort in the unerring promises and the never-ending faithfulness of your Lord.

Let a man go away or come back:
God never leaves. He is always at hand and
if he cannot get into your life, still he is
never farther away than the door.

Meister Eckhart

Tell of His wondrous faithfulness
And sound His pow'r abroad;
Sing the sweet promise of His grace,
The love and truth of God.

Isaac Watts

God's faithfulness has never depended on
the faithfulness of his children....
God is greater than our weakness.
In fact, I think, it is our weakness
that reveals how great God is.

Max Lucado

In God's faithfulness
lies eternal security.

–

Corrie ten Boom

A Prayer

Your faithfulness, Lord, is everlasting.
You are faithful to me even when
I am not faithful to You. Today, let me
serve You with my heart, my soul,
and my mind. And, then, let me rest in
the knowledge of Your unchanging
and constant love for me.
Amen

5

The Shepherding Heart of God

I am the good shepherd.
The good shepherd gives His life
for the sheep.
John 10:11 NKJV

The heart of God is a shepherd's heart. Shepherds were known for the sacrificial care they gave to their flocks. No matter how unpleasant the weather, the shepherd was there to care for his sheep. If a sheep became lost, the shepherd left those who were safe and went out to find the one in trouble. When fresh pasture or clean water was needed, it was the shepherd that led the way. When danger appeared on the horizon, it was this servant of the sheep who stood between his flock and whatever it was that threatened the animals under his care. Sometimes that meant even putting his own life on the line. But that's what a good shepherd did.

Jesus Christ is the supreme good shepherd who always cares for His flock. Others might serve as His under-shepherds and, as such, should be respected. But the ultimate care of the flock rests with the shepherd heart of our God.

Do you have a need? Then look to your Shepherd. Are you feeling threatened or insecure? Then look to the Caretaker of the flock. Whatever the circumstances, you can trust the One who has a shepherd's heart. He has already laid down His life for you. Would He deny you anything less?

God passionately yearns to be in a loving
relationship with the people He created.

Bill Hybels

It was not the soldiers who killed him, nor
the screams of the mob: It was his devotion to us.

Max Lucado

Back when the sacred authors used the imagery
of the shepherd to depict Jesus, they had
a clear understanding of the job description.
A shepherd is needed only when there are
no fences. He is someone who stays with
his sheep at all cost, guiding, protecting, and
walking with them through the fields.
He's not just a person who raises sheep.

Lena Wolter

The Lord my pasture shall prepare,
and feed me with a shepherd's care;
His presence shall my wants supply,
and guard me with a watchful eye.

—

Joseph Addison

A Prayer

*Dear God, You are not only the Good
Shepherd, You are my Good Shepherd.
Help me to trust You with all my needs,
and learn to follow You wherever You
would lead. When danger threatens,
may I run to You and find safety
and protection.*
Amen

6

The Forgiving Heart of God

If we confess our sins,
He is faithful and just
to forgive us our sins and
to cleanse us from
all unrighteousness.
1 John 1:9 NKJV

The heart of God is a forgiving heart. He loves to forgive. We may have just made the biggest mistake of our life, but God will still forgive us. Sin grieves God's heart, but God loves to forgive even in the midst of His grief.

The word forgive means "to release." To forgive is to let go of a debt. It means to not demand payment of a debt. Somebody hurts you, and instead of retaliating, you say to God, "I give this hurt to You. I release it. It's off my shoulders. God, You do with it whatever You want." Real forgiveness is when you say, "It's no longer my business; it's God's. I'm not going to collect on the debt."

In Luke 23, we find Jesus on the cross. Crucified with Him are two criminals, one on His right and one on His left. Jesus is dying with thieves, men who are the outcasts of society. He's hanging on a cross between two men who belong there—but He doesn't! And amazingly, Jesus says, "Father, forgive them, for they do not know what they do" (v. 34). I have always been amazed by that verse. Jesus was hanging on the cross absolutely and totally innocent, asking the Father to forgive people who were not innocent. When people were at their worst, Jesus was at His best, saying, "Father, forgive them."

If you've been to Calvary and received the forgiveness of God, then adopt the heart of God and let the forgiven become a forgiver. And remember: There's nothing more tender than the forgiving heart of God.

There is nothing that God cannot forgive except for the rejection of Christ. No matter how black the sin, how hideous the sin, if we but confess it to Him in true repentance and faith, He will forgive. He will accept and forgive.

Ruth Bell Graham

God is glorified when people believe His gospel, love His son, and accept His diagnosis of their greatest need, which is forgiveness of sin.

John MacArthur

Where is the foolish person who would think it in his power to commit a sin more than God could forgive?

—

St. Francis of Sales

A Prayer

Father, forgiveness is Your commandment, and I know that I need to forgive others just as You have forgiven me. But genuine, lasting forgiveness is difficult. Help me to forgive those who have injured me, and deliver me from the traps of anger and bitterness. Sometimes, I feel the strong desire to strike out against those who have hurt me, but You command me to turn away from revenge. Keep me mindful, Lord, that I am never fully liberated until I have been freed from the prison of hatred—and that You offer me that freedom through Your Son, Jesus Christ.

Amen

7

The Jealous Heart of God

For you shall worship no other god,
for the LORD,
whose name is Jealous,
is a jealous God.
Exodus 34:14 NKJV

*O*ur loving Heavenly Father is a compassionate God who seeks the very best for us. Because of this, however, our Creator is also a jealous God who intends that we worship Him and only Him. God's jealousy, however, should not be interpreted as a sign that God is uncaring or sinister. God's jealousy is a righteous jealousy for His people. God wants this: He wants that we not be robbed of that which is best. And that which is best is this: nothing other than God.

It makes the heart of God jealous when we make gods out of anything but Him. It makes the heart of God jealous when our possessions possess us. God is jealous for our attention, for our love, and for our worship. Because He is an egomanic? No! On the contrary, He wants us to receive the very best—*Him!*

May we, as believers who have been saved by the blood of a risen Christ, recognize that what God has to offer is the very best—and make our decisions accordingly.

Even God attributes to himself avarice, jealousy, anger; and these are virtues as well as kindness, pity, constancy.

Blaise Pascal

When properly understood, [God's] jealousy isn't inconsistent with His love and holiness; it's required by it. When we react against the Bible's description of God as a jealous God, we forget that there are times when jealousy is right and appropriate.

Dan Vander Lugt

For the LORD your God is a consuming fire, a jealous God.

Deuteronomy 4:24 NKJV

God knows that the best possible thing *for us* is to be absolutely taken up and obsessed with him. He knows that he's the ultimate source of all our joy and comfort, and wants us to come to the source.

—

Mike Taylor

A Prayer

Dear Lord, You are right in Your jealousy. I will have no other Gods before You. You sent Your Son, Jesus, to die on a cross for my sins. Jesus endured indignity, suffering, and death so that I might live. Because He lives, I, too, have Your promise of eternal life. Let me share this Good News, Lord, with a world that so desperately needs Your healing hand and the salvation of Your Son. Amen

8

The Humble Heart of God

Let this mind be in you which was also in Christ Jesus, who, being in the form of God, did not consider it robbery to be equal with God, but made Himself of no reputation, taking the form of a bondservant, and coming in the likeness of men. And being found in appearance as a man, He humbled Himself and became obedient to the point of death, even the death of the cross.

Philippians 2:5–8 NKJV

*I*t's not unusual for God's sovereignty to be borne through humility. Consider God's sovereignty and the humility that is found in the person of Jesus Christ. It almost seems like they contradict each other. In Jesus, we have the sovereign God—who humbles Himself. The *sovereign* God has a *humble* heart. What a remarkable truth!

Philippians 2:5-8 details the humble heart of God. Each phrase is significant. The passage starts with, "Let this mind be in you which was also in Christ Jesus, who, being in the form of God...." The word that is translated as "form" speaks of a *change* in form. Some translations use the word "nature" here. But the verse is not talking about God's nature; it's talking about the form in which we perceive God's nature. Nature describes essence; form describes how we view that essence. The word here clearly means the form of God, not the nature of God. To be sure, Jesus, is by nature, God. But this phrase speaks of Jesus being in the form of God and then changing.

John tells us that God is spirit (John 4:24). Apparently, we are to understand that before Jesus became a man, He was of that same form. The writer of Philippians goes on: Jesus, being in the form of God, "did not consider it robbery to be equal with God." Other versions of the Bible translate this, "did not consider equality with God something to be grasped" (NIV). I think "grasped" is a better translation here. The word means to lay your hands on something, to cling to. Jesus, in the form of God, did not think that form was something He had to tenaciously cling to in order to be God. In other words, He could give up the free form of a spirit and still be God; He could take a body of flesh and remain equally God. He didn't need to cling to the form of God in order to retain what it means to be God.

So Christ gave up that form and "He made Himself of no reputation." He "made Himself nothing" (NIV). The idea here is that of "emptying." Jesus emptied Himself and came to earth to live among us and die. The Giver of Life, the One who created life, the sovereign God submitted Himself to obedience and death, but not just any old death, not a quiet death during His sleep, or a wayward donkey accident. He submitted Himself to death, "even the death of the cross," the most cruel, violent, wicked, abominable death known to mankind.

Marvel at the humble heart of God!

Humility is the exhibition of
the spirit of Jesus Christ and
is the touchstone of saintliness.

–

Oswald Chambers

A Prayer

*Heavenly Father, Jesus clothed Himself
with humility when He chose to come
to this earth so that He might live and
die for all creation. Christ is my Master
and my example. Clothe me
with humility, Lord, so that I might be
more like Your Son.*

Amen

9

The Rejoicing Heart of God

And as the bridegroom rejoices
over the bride, so shall
your God rejoice over you.
Isaiah 62:5 NKJV

My grandfather was a Baptist deacon. He was a simple man, an electrician by trade. He was a simple, godly electrician. And he used to say something that I haven't heard in a long time. "No Bible, no breakfast!" Those words are still right on target. When we, like my grandfather, place our love for God above our own personal desires, God rejoices!

When the Lord is in the midst of a people who worship Him in a spirit of humility and love, His heart overflows with joy. The psalmist says it this way:

The Lord your God in your midst,
The Mighty One, will save;
He will rejoice over you with gladness,
He will quiet you with His love,
He will rejoice over you with singing.
Zephaniah 3:17 NKJV

Do you sincerely want God to rejoice over you? Then live righteously. Allow God to preside over every aspect of your life. And what you'll find is that it's a two-way street. As you give God reason to rejoice over you, you will find your own heart filled with joy.

Why not get started today? Ask God to show you a specific way you can cause His heart to rejoice.

Our obedience does not make God any bigger
or better than He already is. Anything God
commands of us is so that our joy may be full—
the joy of seeing His glory revealed to us and in us!

Beth Moore

*God has spoken in His holiness:
"I will rejoice; I will divide Shechem and
measure out the Valley of Succoth."*

Psalm 60:6 NKJV

Joy can be the echo of God's life within you.

Duane Pederson

Christ and joy go together.

E. Stanley Jones

All movements of discipleship arrive
at a place where joy is experienced.
Every step of assent toward God develops
the capacity to enjoy. Not only is there,
increasingly, more to be enjoyed,
there is steadily the acquired ability
to enjoy it.

—

Eugene Peterson

A Prayer

*Dear Lord, it is my heart's desire to live
in such a way that You can rejoice over
me. May You develop in me through
Your Holy Spirit, those things that would
bring joy to Your heart. And as You rejoice,
may I also feel the joy of Your pleasure.
May I rejoice with You and give You
the praise and the glory forever.
Amen*

10

The Grace-filled Heart of God

My grace is sufficient for you, for My strength is made perfect in weakness.
2 Corinthians 12:9 NKJV

$\mathcal{T}$he grace of God overflows from His heart. And if we open our hearts to Him, we receive His grace, and we are blessed with joy, abundance, peace, and eternal life.

The familiar words of Ephesians 2:8 make God's promise perfectly clear: "For by grace you have been saved through faith, and that not of yourselves; it is the gift of God" (NKJV). In other words, we are saved, not by our actions, but by God's mercy. We are saved, not because of our good deeds, but because of our faith in Christ.

God's grace is the ultimate gift, a gift beyond comprehension and beyond compare. And because it is the ultimate gift, we owe God the ultimate in thanksgiving.

God's grace is indeed a gift from the heart—*God's heart*. And as believers, we must accept God's precious gift thankfully, humbly, and immediately—today is never too soon because tomorrow may be too late.

The grace of God runs downhill toward
the ones who are emptied and vulnerable,
toward the ones who admit that they struggle.

Angela Thomas

God's grace and power seem to reach their peak
when we are at our weakest point.

Anne Graham Lotz

Yes, God's grace is always sufficient,
and His arms are always open to give it.
But, will our arms be open to receive it?

Beth Moore

Grace grows best in the winter.

C. H. Spurgeon

Grace comes from the heart of a gracious God who wants to stun you and overwhelm you with a gift you don't deserve— salvation, adoption, a spiritual ability to use in kingdom service, answered prayer, the church, His presence, His wisdom, His guidance, His love.

—

Bill Hybels

A Prayer

Accepting Your grace can be hard, Lord. Somehow, I feel that I must earn Your love and Your acceptance. Yet, the Bible makes this glorious promise: You love me and save me by Your grace. It is a gift I can only accept and not earn. Thank You, Dear Lord, for Your gift of grace.

Amen

11

The Guiding Heart of God

In all your ways acknowledge Him,
and He shall direct your paths.
Proverbs 3:6 NKJV

*W*hen we genuinely seek to know the heart of God—when we prayerfully seek His wisdom and His will—our Heavenly Father carefully guides us over the peaks and valleys of life. And as Christians, we can be comforted: Whether we find ourselves at the pinnacle of the mountain or the darkest depths of the valley, the loving heart of God is always there with us.

As Christians whose salvation has been purchased by the blood of Christ, we have every reason to live joyously and courageously. After all, Christ has already fought and won our battle for us—He did so on the cross at Calvary. But despite Christ's sacrifice, and despite God's promises, we may become confused or disoriented by the endless complications and countless distractions of life here in the 21st century.

If you're unsure of your next step, lean upon God's promises and lift your prayers to Him. Remember that God is always near; remember that He is your protector and your deliverer. Open yourself to His heart, and trust Him to guide your path. When you do, the guiding heart of God will direct your steps, and you will receive His blessings today, tomorrow, and throughout eternity.

God will prove to you how good and acceptable
and perfect His will is when He's got His hands
on the steering wheel of your life.

Stuart and Jill Briscoe

It's a bit like river rafting with an experienced
guide. You may begin to panic when the guide
steers you straight into a steep waterfall,
especially if another course appears much safer.
Yet, after you've emerged from the swirling depths
and wiped the spray from your eyes, you see that
just beyond the seemingly "safe" route was
a series of jagged rocks. Your guide knew
what he was doing after all.

Shirley Dobson

The Bible is not a guidebook to a theological
museum. It is a road map showing us the way
into neglected or even forgotten glories
of the living God.

Raymond Ortlund

Make my path sure, O Lord.
Establish my goings. Send me when
and where You will and manifest
to all that Thou are my guide.

—

Jim Elliot

A Prayer

*Lord, You have a plan for my life
that is grander than I can imagine.
Let Your purposes be my purposes.
Let Your will be my will. When I am
confused, give me clarity. When I am
frightened, give me courage. Let me be
Your faithful servant, always seeking
Your guidance for my life. And let me
always be a shining beacon for
Your Son, Christ Jesus, today
and every day that I live.
Amen*

12

The Loving Heart of God

For I am persuaded that neither death nor life, nor angels nor principalities nor powers, nor things present nor things to come, nor height nor depth, nor any other created thing, shall be able to separate us from the love of God which is in Christ Jesus our Lord.

Romans 8:38, 39 NKJV

The words of 1 John 4:8 teach us that "He who does not love does not know God, for God is love" (NKJV). And because we can be assured that God is love, we can also be assured that God's heart is a loving heart.

God loves you. He loves you more than you can imagine; His affection is deeper than you can fathom. God made you in His own image and gave you salvation through the person of His Son, Jesus Christ. And as a result, you have an important decision to make. You must decide what to do about God's love: you can return it . . . or not.

When you accept the love that flows from the heart of God, you are transformed. When you embrace God's love, you feel differently about yourself, your neighbors, your community, your church, and your world. When you open your heart to God's love, you will feel compelled to share God's message—and His compassion—with others.

God's heart is overflowing with love . . . for you. Accept that love. Return that love. And share that love. Today.

"O Love that will not let me go,
I rest my weary soul in Thee;
I give Thee back the life I owe, that,
in Thine ocean depths, its flow
May richer, fuller be!"

George Matheson

Christianity does not think of a man finally
submitting to the power of God, it thinks of him
as finally surrendering to the love of God.
It is not that man's will is crushed,
but that man's heart is broken.

William Barclay

As the sun shines on all things on earth in
the same way, yet as if each is separate,
that is how God's love is for each of us:
the same yet unique.

St. Thérèse of Lisieux

Abandon yourself utterly for the love of God,
and in this way you will become truly happy.

St. Henry Suso

Incomprehensible and immutable is the love
of God. For it was not after we were reconciled to
him by the blood of his Son that he began
to love us, but he loved us before the foundation
of the world, that with his only begotten Son
we too might be sons of God
before we were any thing at all.
St. Augustine

A Prayer

*Thank You, Lord, for Your love. Your love
is boundless, infinite, and eternal. Today, let me
pause and reflect upon Your love for me, and
let me share that love with all those who cross
my path. And, as an expression of my love for You,
Father, let me share the saving message of
Your Son, Jesus with a world in desperate need
of His peace.
Amen*

13

The All-knowing Heart of God

For there is not a word on my tongue,
but behold, O LORD,
You know it altogether.
Psalm 139:4 NKJV

The heart of God is all-knowing. Even when nobody else is watching, God is watching. Even when we believe that the consequences of our actions will be known only to ourselves, our Creator sees our actions, and He responds accordingly. Ours is a God who, in His own time and in His own way, rewards righteousness and punishes sin. It's as simple as that.

Nothing that we say or do escapes the watchful eye of our Lord. God understands that we are not perfect, and He understands that we will inevitably make mistakes, but He wants us to live according to His rules, not our own. And when we don't, He does not protect us from the natural consequences of our mistakes.

The next time that you're tempted to say something that you shouldn't say or do something that you shouldn't do, remember that you can't keep secrets from the all-knowing heart of God. So don't even try!

God knows instantly and effortlessly all matter
and all matters, all mind and every mind,
all spirit and all spirits, all being and every being,
all creaturehood and all creatures, every plurality
and all pluralities, all law and every law,
all relations, all causes, all thoughts,
all mysteries, all enigmas, all feeling, all desires,
every unuttered secret, all thrones and dominions,
all personalities, all things visible and invisible
in heaven and in earth, motion, space, time, life,
death, good, evil, heaven, and hell.

A. W. Tozer

Anyone can count the seeds in an apple,
but only God can count the number of apples
in a seed.

Robert Schuller

What can escape the eye of God, all seeing,
Or deceive his heart, omniscient?

John Milton

Before God created the universe,
he already had you in mind.

Erwin Lutzer

Our heavenly Father wants nothing
but the best for any of us,
and only He knows what that is,
for He is All-wise, the Omniscient.

—

Elisabeth Elliot

A Prayer

*Dear Lord, You are the source of
all wisdom, and You are my Teacher.
I will study Your Word, and I will seek
Your will. Today, I will stand upon
the truth that You reveal, and I will
share Your wisdom with my family,
with my friends, and with the world.
Amen*

14

The Peace-giving Heart of God

But now in Christ Jesus you who once were far off have been brought near by the blood of Christ. For He Himself is our peace.
Ephesians 2:13, 14 NKJV

he beautiful words of John 14:27 remind us that the heart of God is the source of our peace: "Peace I leave with you, My peace I give to you; not as the world gives do I give to you. Let not your heart be troubled, neither let it be afraid." Jesus offers us peace, not as the world gives, but as He alone gives. We, as believers, can accept His peace or ignore it.

When we accept the peace of Jesus Christ into our hearts, our lives are transformed. And then, because we possess the gift of peace, we can share that gift with fellow Christians, family members, friends, and associates. If, on the other hand, we choose to ignore the gift of peace—for whatever reason—we cannot share what we do not possess.

Today, as a gift to yourself, to your family, and to your friends, claim the inner peace that is your spiritual birthright: the peace of Jesus Christ. It is offered freely; it has been paid for in full; it is yours for the asking. So ask. And then share.

Peace does not mean to be in a place where there is no noise, trouble, or hard work. Peace means to be in the midst of all those things and still be calm in your heart.

Catherine Marshall

It is what Jesus is, not what we are, that gives rest to the soul. If we really want to overcome Satan and have peace with God, we must "fix our eyes on Jesus." Let his death, his suffering, his glories, and his intercession be fresh on your mind.

C. H. Spurgeon

The better you become acquainted with God, the less tensions you feel and the more peace you possess.

Charles L. Allen

A great many people are trying to make peace, but that has already been done. God has not left it for us to do; all we have to do is to enter into it.

D. L. Moody

I believe that in every time and
place it is within our power to
acquiesce in the will of God—
and what peace it brings to do so!

–

Elisabeth Elliot

A Prayer

*The world talks about peace,
but only You, Lord, can give a perfect
and lasting peace. True peace comes
through the Prince of Peace, and
His peace passes all understanding.
Help me to accept His peace—
and share it—this day and forever.
Amen*

15

The Purpose-filled Heart of God

*And we know that all things work
together for good to those
who love God,
to those who are the called
according to His purpose.*

Romans 8:28 NKJV

*G*od has a plan for your life—a plan that is near and dear to His heart. If you genuinely seek to fulfill God's plan for your life, then you must do this: you must make decisions that are pleasing to Him. The most important decision of your life is, of course, your commitment to accept God's Son as your personal Lord and Savior. And, once your eternal destiny is secured, you will undoubtedly ask yourself the question "What now, Lord?" If you earnestly seek God's will, you will find it...in time.

Life is best lived on purpose. And purpose, like everything else in the universe, begins in the heart of God. Whether you realize it or not, God has a direction for your life, a divine calling, a path along which He intends to lead you. When you welcome God into your heart and establish a genuine relationship with Him, He will begin—and He will continue—to make His purposes known.

Sometimes, God's intentions will be clear to you; other times, God's plan will seem uncertain at best. But even on those difficult days when you are unsure which way to turn, you must never lose sight of these overriding facts: God created you for a reason; He has important work for you to do; and He's waiting patiently for you to do it. So why not begin today?

The Christian life is one of faith, where we find
ourselves routinely overdriving our headlights
but knowing it's okay because God is in control
and has a purpose behind it.

Bill Hybels

When the dream of our heart is one that God has
planted there, a strange happiness flows into us.
At that moment, all of the spiritual resources of
the universe are released to help us. Our praying
is then at one with the will of God and becomes
a channel for the Creator's purposes
for us and our world.

Catherine Marshall

Nothing can reach us, from any source in earth
or hell, no matter how evil, which God cannot turn
to His own redemptive purpose. Let us be glad
that the way is not a game of chance—
it is a way appointed for God's eternal glory
and our final good.

Elisabeth Elliot

God has His reasons. He has His purposes. Ours is an intentional God, brimming over with motive and mission. He never does things capriciously or decides with the flip of a coin

—

Joni Eareckson Tada

A Prayer
Dear Lord, let Your purposes be my purposes. Let Your priorities be my priorities. Let Your will be my will. Let Your Word be my guide. And, let me grow in faith and in wisdom today and every day.
Amen

16

The Diligent Heart of God

*Being confident of this very thing,
that He who has begun a good work
in you will complete it until
the day of Jesus Christ.*
Philippians 1:6 NKJV

*W*hen many of us look back on our lives we can see projects left only half completed, relationships that had potential but didn't quite get off the ground, good intentions that were never acted upon—but not God. God has never started something that He hasn't finished. His workmanship is the product of a diligent heart—a heart committed to finishing what He began.

The diligent heart of God is clearly demonstrated by God's commitment to each of us. This commitment was declared most dramatically by the gift of His Son. Romans 5:8 tells us, "But God demonstrates His own love toward us, in that while we were still sinners, Christ died for us." Having paid that tremendous price for us, you can be sure that God is not going to give up on you until His good work is completed on the day of Jesus Christ.

Are you worried that God will give up on you? Have you thought that maybe God has washed His hands of you in disgust? Then put those fears to rest. Through thick and thin, God is going to hang in there with you until the great work He began in you on the day that you accepted Christ as your Savior is finished. His diligent heart will not allow Him to do any less.

God created us, not because He needed us,
but because He wanted us.
The act was based on the pleasure of His will.

Beth Moore

We ought then, beloved brothers,
to remember and to know, that when we call
God Father, we ought to act as God's children.
Then, He can take as much pleasure in
considering us His sons as we do
in thinking of Him as our Father.

St. Cyprian of Carthage

If you aim at and seek after nothing but
the pleasure of God and the welfare of
your neighbor, you will enjoy freedom within.

Thomas à Kempis

Any patch of sunlight in a woods will show
you something about the sun which you could
never get from reading books on astronomy.
These pure and spontaneous pleasures are
"patches of Godlight"

in the woods of our experience.

—

C. S. Lewis

A Prayer

*Dear Lord, I thank You that You never leave
anything undone. I rejoice that at
the Day of the Lord Jesus, I will be made
complete and whole. Until that day, I thank
You that You are at work in my life through
Your Holy Spirit and that He will guide
and direct me as You transform me
into the image of Your Son, Jesus.
Amen*

17

The Awesome Heart of God

Ah, Lord GOD! Behold,
You have made the heavens
and the earth by Your
great power and outstretched arm.
There is nothing too hard for You.
Jeremiah 32:17 NKJV

*T*he expression "awesome" has become a catch phrase in our society. We say that this is awesome and that is awesome, but, in reality, there is only one thing that truly can claim that title—God. No where is God's awesomeness reflected more intimately than in the awesome love that flows from His heart to ours. God's ability to love is not burdened by boundaries or by limitations. The love that flows from His awesome heart is infinite and beyond our comprehension.

But even though we cannot fully *understand* the awesome heart of God, we *can* praise it, worship it, and marvel at its mercy.

When we worship God with faith and assurance, when we place Him at the absolute center of our lives, we invite His love into our hearts. In turn, we grow to love Him more deeply as we sense His love for us. Augustine wrote, "I love you, Lord, not doubtingly, but with absolute certainty. Your Word beat upon my heart until I fell in love with you, and now the universe and everything in it tells me to love you."

Let us pray that we, too, will turn our hearts to the Creator, knowing with certainty that His awesome heart has ample room for each of us, and that we, in turn, must make room in our hearts for Him.

He upholds the whole creation, founded
the earth, and still sustains it by the word of
his power. What cannot he do in the affairs of
families and kingdoms, far beyond our conception
and expectation, who hangs the earth
upon nothing?

Matthew Henry

Our evangelical culture tends to take the awesome
reality of a transcendent God who is worthy to be
feared and downsize Him so He could fit into our
"buddy system." The way we talk about Him,
the way we pray, and, more strikingly, the way we
live shows that we have somehow lost our sense
of being appropriately awestruck in the presence
of a holy and all-powerful God.

Joseph Stowell

Our God is an awesome God. There is thunder in
his footsteps and lightning in his fists.

Rich Mullins

An awe for the composer, God,
is necessary before a person can fully
understand his score, the Bible.

—

Fred Smith

A Prayer

*Dear Lord, for the love You have shown
me and the blessings You have
given me, I stand in awe of You.
Your Son died so that I might receive
the blessing of eternal love and eternal
life. I will praise You today, tomorrow,
and forever, Lord, for Your love,
for Your mercy, and for Your Son.
Amen*

18

The Transcendent Heart of God

*For the eyes of the LORD run to and fro
throughout the whole earth,
to show Himself strong on behalf
of those whose heart is loyal to Him.*
2 Chronicles 16:9 NKJV

*H*ave you ever thought that God's heart transcends time and space? It reaches beyond the stars, and it reaches into the darkest, smallest corner of every human being.

God sees *everything* (Job 28:24). And when God sees you reach out to Him, He responds (Psalm 145:18)—no "ifs, ands, or buts," and no waiting in line for a ticket.

The words of Romans 8 make this promise: "For I am persuaded that neither death nor life, nor angels nor principalities nor powers, nor things present nor things to come, nor height nor depth, nor any other created thing, shall be able to separate us from the love of God which is in Christ Jesus our Lord" (38, 39 NKJV).

Take God at His word and welcome His Son into your heart. When you do, God's transcendent love will surround you and transform you, now and forever.

God is in all things and in every place. There is not a place in the world in which he is not most truly present. Just as birds, wherever they fly, always meet with the air, so we, wherever we go, or wherever we are, always find God present.

St. Francis de Sales

Begin where we will, God is there first.

A. W. Tozer

A philosopher once asked, "Where is God?"
The Christian answered,
"Let me first ask you, where is he not?"

John Arrowsmith

A sense of deity is inscribed on every heart.

John Calvin

To adore is to be drawn away from my own preoccupations and into the presence of Jesus. It means letting go of what I want, what I desire, and what I have planned;
it means fully trusting Jesus and his love.

—

Henri Nouwen

A Prayer

Dear God, You are nearer to me than the air that I breathe. Help me to feel Your presence in every situation and in every circumstance. You are with me, Lord, in times of celebration and in times of sorrow. You are with me when I am strong and when I am weak. You never leave my side, even when it seems to me that You are far away. Today and every day, Dear God, let me feel You and acknowledge Your presence so that others, too, might come to know You through me.
Amen

19

The Unwavering Heart of God

*For He is the living God,
and steadfast forever;*
Daniel 6:26 NKJV

*G*od is steadfast in His willingness to protect us. We, in turn, must be steadfast in our willingness to be protected! In other words, we must willingly accept the protection that flows freely from the unwavering heart of God. This point is illustrated by the familiar story found in Mark 4: 35–41: When a terrible storm rose quickly on the Sea of Galilee, the disciples were afraid. Although they had witnessed many miracles, the disciples feared for their lives, so they turned to Jesus, and He calmed the waters and the wind.

Sometimes, we, like the disciples, feel threatened by the storms of life. When we are fearful, we, too, can turn to Christ for comfort and for courage. In life's darkest moments, we can depend upon the unwavering love of our perfect Heavenly Father.

The next time you find yourself facing a fear-provoking situation, remember that the One who calmed the wind and the waves is also your personal Savior. Then ask yourself which is stronger: your faith or your fear. The answer should be obvious: Whatever your challenge, God can handle it. Your job is to let Him.

God is the great reality. His resources are
available and endless. His promises are
real and glorious, beyond our wildest dreams.

J. B. Phillips

We must depend upon the performance of
the promise when all the doors
leading up to it are shut.

Matthew Henry

The Lord may not come when you want him,
but he's always going to be there on time.

Lou Gossett, Jr.

The stars may fall, but God's promises
will stand and be fulfilled.

J. I. Packer

God does not give us everything
we want, but He does fulfill all
His promises as He leads us along
the best and straightest paths
to Himself.

—

Dietrich Bonhoeffer

A Prayer

*Heavenly Father, sometimes I am
troubled, and sometimes I grow
weary. When I am weak, Lord, give
me strength. When I am discouraged,
renew me. When I am fearful, let me
feel Your healing touch. Let me always
trust in Your steadfastness, Lord, and
let me draw strength from knowing that
You are always there for me.*
Amen

20

The Protective Heart of God

*As for God, His way is perfect;
the word of the LORD is proven;
He is a shield to all
who trust in Him.*
Psalm 18:30 NKJV

*B*ecause we are imperfect human beings living imperfect lives, we worry. Even though we, as Christians, have the assurance of salvation—even though we, as believers, have the promise of God's love and protection—we find ourselves fretting over the countless details of everyday life. Jesus understood our concerns, and He addressed them.

In Matthew 6, Jesus makes it clear that the heart of God is a protective, caring heart:

Therefore I say to you, do not worry about your life, what you will eat or what you will drink; nor about your body, what you will put on. Is not life more than food and the body more than clothing? Look at the birds of the air, for they neither sow nor reap nor gather into barns; yet your heavenly Father feeds them. Are you not of more value than they? Which of you by worrying can add one cubit to his stature? . . . Therefore do not worry about tomorrow, for tomorrow will worry about its own things. Sufficient for the day is its own trouble. (25-27, 34)

Perhaps you are uncertain about your future, your finances, your relationships, or your health. Or perhaps you are simply a "worrier" by nature. If so, make Matthew 6 a regular part of your daily Bible reading. This beautiful passage will remind you that God still sits in His heaven and you are His beloved child. Then, perhaps, you will worry a little less and trust God a little more, and that's as it should be because God is trustworthy...and you are protected.

A God wise enough to create me and the world I live in is wise enough to watch out for me.

Philip Yancey

God delights in spreading His protective wings and enfolding His frightened, weary, beaten-down, worn-out children.

Bill Hybels

Who is it that is your Shepherd? The Lord!
Oh, my friends, what a wonderful announcement!
The Lord God of heaven and earth, and Almighty
Creator of all things, He who holds the universe in
His hand as though it were a very little thing.
He is your shepherd and has charged Himself
with the care and keeping of you, as a shepherd is
charged with the care and keeping of his sheep.
If your hearts could really take in this thought,
you would never have a fear or a care again,
for with such a Shepherd how could it be possible
for you ever to want for any good thing?

—

Hannah Whitall Smith

A Prayer

Thank You, Dear Lord, for Your protection.
In a dangerous world, I rejoice to know that
Your heart is concerned with my well-being.
Amen

21

The Sovereign Heart of God

*Let the heavens rejoice,
and let the earth be glad;
and let them say among the nations,
"The LORD reigns."*
1 Chronicles 16:31 NKJV

*T*he heart of God is sovereign: it reigns over all God's creation, including you. Your challenge is to recognize God's sovereignty and live in accordance with His commandments. Sometimes, of course, this is easier said than done.

Proverbs 3:6 gives you guidance: "In all your ways acknowledge Him, and He shall direct your paths." When you think about it, the words in this verse make a powerful promise: If you acknowledge God's sovereignty over every aspect of your life, He will guide your path. That's an important promise. So, as you prayerfully consider the path that God intends for you to take, here are things you should do: You should study His Word and be ever-watchful for His signs. You should associate with fellow believers who will encourage your spiritual growth. You should listen carefully to that inner voice that speaks to you in the quiet moments of your daily devotionals. And, as you continually seek God's unfolding purpose for your life, you should be patient.

Your Heavenly Father may not always reveal Himself as quickly as you would like. But rest assured: God is sovereign. At the right time, in the right way, His sovereign heart will bring to pass what is right.

Knowing God's sovereignty and unconditional love
imparts a beauty to life...and to you.

Kay Arthur

Jesus did not promise to change
the circumstances around us. He promised
great peace and pure joy to those who would learn
to believe that God actually controls all things.

Corrie ten Boom

Waiting is the hardest kind of work,
but God knows best,
and we may joyfully leave all in His hands.

Lottie Moon

When terrible things happen, there are two
choices, and only two: We can trust God, or
we can defy Him. We believe that God is God,
He's still got the whole world in His hands and
knows exactly what He's doing, or we must believe
that He is not God and that we are at
the awful mercy of mere chance.

Elisabeth Elliot

God's sovereignty is the attribute
by which He rules His entire creation, and
to be sovereign, God must be all-knowing,
all-powerful, and absolutely free.

—

A.W. Tozer

A Prayer

*Lord, when my path is steep and my heart
is troubled, let me trust in You.
When I become discouraged or anxious,
let me depend upon You. When I lose faith
in this world, let me never lose faith in You.
Remind me, Lord, that in every situation and
in every season of life, You will love me and
protect me. And, with You as my protector,
Lord, I need never lose hope because You
remain sovereign today and forever.
Amen*

22

The Sufficient Heart of God

*And my God shall supply
all your need according to His riches
in glory by Christ Jesus.*
Philippians 4:19 NKJV

*O*f this you can be sure: the loving heart of God is sufficient to meet your needs. No matter what dangers you may face or heartbreaks you must endure, God is with you. And He stands ready to provide for whatever you truly need.

The Psalmist writes, "Weeping may endure for a night, but joy comes in the morning" (Psalm 30:5 NKJV). But when we are suffering, the morning may seem very far away. It is not. God promises that He is "near to those who have a broken heart" (Psalm 34:18 NKJV). In times of intense sadness, we must turn to Him, and we must encourage our friends and family members to find their sufficiency in Him as well.

If you are experiencing the intense pain of a recent loss, or if you are still mourning a loss from long ago, perhaps you are now ready to begin the next stage of your journey with God. If so, be mindful of this fact: the loving heart of God is sufficient to meet any challenge, including yours. Trust the sufficient heart of God.

He who has God and many other things has
no more than he who has God alone.

C. S. Lewis

I grew up learning to be self-reliant, but now,
to grow up in Christ, I must unlearn self-reliance
and learn self-distrust in light of his all-sufficiency.

Mary Morrison Suggs

The last and greatest lesson that the soul has
to learn is the fact that God, and God alone,
is enough for all its needs. This is the lesson
that all His dealings with us are meant to teach;
and this is the crowning discovery of
our whole Christian life. God is enough!

Hannah Whitall Smith

Like Paul, we may bear thorns so that we can
discover God's perfect sufficiency.

Beth Moore

Jesus has been consistently
affectionate and true to us.
He has shared his great wealth with us.
How can we doubt the all-powerful,
all-sufficient Lord?

—

C. H. Spurgeon

A Prayer

*You have promised, Lord, that You will
not give me any more than I can bear.
You have promised to lift me out of my
grief and despair. You have promised to
put a new song on my lips. I thank You,
Lord, for Your sufficiency. Restore me;
heal me; and use me as You will.*
Amen

23

The Willful Heart of God

Teach me to do Your will,
for You are my God;
Your Spirit is good.
Lead me in the land
of uprightness.
Psalm 143:10 NKJV

*G*od has a plan for our world and our lives. God does not do things by accident; He is willful and intentional. Unfortunately for us, we simply cannot always understand the willful heart of God. Why? Because we are mortal beings with limited understanding. Thus, we can never fully comprehend the will of God. But as believers in a benevolent Heavenly Father, we must always trust the will of God.

Before His crucifixion, Jesus went to the Mount of Olives and poured out His heart to God (Luke 22). Jesus knew of the agony that He was destined to endure, but He also knew that God's will must be done. We, like our Savior, face trials that bring fear and trembling to the very depths of our souls. But like Christ, we, too, must ultimately seek God's will, not our own.

As this day unfolds, seek God's will and obey His Word. When you entrust your life to Him completely and without reservation, He will give you the strength to meet any challenge, the courage to face any trial, and the wisdom to live in His righteousness and in His peace.

Doing God's will is never hard.
The only thing that is hard is not doing His will.

Oswald Chambers

True faith does not so much attempt to manipulate
God to do our will as it does to position us
to do his will.

Philip Yancey

Praying effectively requires the intervention
of God's Holy Spirit. Through the intentions
of our hearts and the engagement of the Spirit,
we discover the will of God.

Shirley Dobson

No one may prefer his own will to the will of God,
but in everything we must seek and
do the will of God.

St. Basil the Great

God alone is in control of circumstances.
You are safer in a famine *in His will*
than in a palace *out of His will*.

—

Warren Wiersbe

A Prayer

*Dear Lord, You are the Creator of
the universe, and I know that Your plan for
my life is grander than I can imagine. Let
Your purposes be my purposes. Let Your will
be my will. When I am confused, give me
clarity. When I am worried, give me strength.
Let me be Your faithful servant, Lord, always
seeking Your guidance and Your will for
my life. Let me live this day and every day
according to Your commandments and
with the assurance of Your promises,
in Jesus' name I pray.
Amen*

24

The Giving Heart of God

*Every good gift and every
perfect gift is from above
and comes down
from the Father of lights.*
James 1:17 NKJV

*T*he heart of God overflows with gifts for His children, and you are no exception. God has given you a special array of talents and opportunities, and you should be thankful. But you should also beware: neither natural talent nor social position will guarantee your success. Your gifts from God must be cultivated and nurtured; otherwise, they will go unused...and God's gift to you will be squandered.

The gifts that you possess are precious treasures from the Giver of all things good. Do you have a spiritual gift? Share it. Do you have a testimony about the things that Christ has done for you? Don't leave your story untold. Do you possess financial resources? Share them. Do you have particular talents? Hone your skills and use them for God's glory.

When you hoard (or squander) the blessings that God has given you, you are living in rebellion against His commandments. But when you obey God by sharing His gifts freely and without fanfare, you invite Him to bless you more and more.

Today, be a faithful steward of your talents and treasures. And then prepare yourself for even greater blessings that are sure to come.

God is the giver, and we are the receivers.
And His richest gifts are bestowed not upon those
who do the greatest things, but upon those
who accept His abundance and His grace.

Hannah Whitall Smith

We must stir up the gift of God. Like sugar in
the lemonade, it may be there, but
it needs to be set in motion.

Vance Havner

God gives His gifts where He finds the vessel
empty enough to receive them.

C. S. Lewis

One thing taught large in the Holy Scriptures is
that while God gives His gifts freely, He will require
a strict accounting of them at the end of the road.
Each man is personally responsible for his store,
be it large or small, and will be required to explain
his use of it before the judgment seat of Christ.

A.W. Tozer

The Lord has abundantly blessed me all of my life. I'm not trying to pay Him back for all of His wonderful gifts; I just realize that He gave them to me to give away.

—

Lisa Whelchel

A Prayer

Lord, You loved me before I was ever born; You sent Your Son, Jesus, to redeem me from my sins; You have given me the gift of eternal life. I will be thankful always, and I will praise You always. Today, I will share the priceless blessings that I have received: I will share my joy, my possessions, and my faith with others. And I will be a humble giver, Lord, so that all the glory might be Yours. Amen

25

The Helping Heart of God

I will lift up my eyes to the hills.
From whence comes my help?
My help comes from the LORD,
Who made heaven and earth.

Psalm 121:1, 2 NKJV

The heart of God yearns to help His children. But sometimes God's children resist His help by disobeying His commandments. Never allow yourself to fall into that spiritual trap. God's commandments were not given to make life miserable for you. Indeed, just the opposite. They were given to help you avoid many of the pitfalls of life.

God's helping heart yearns to keep His children safe. He longs to help them live full and satisfying lives. Jesus said, "I have come that they may have life, and that they may have it more abundantly" (John 10:10).

Do you want to live an abundant life? Then let God's helping heart show you the way. Study His Word and apply it to your daily life. God's helping heart is as near as your Bible.

"Fear not, I am with thee—O be not dismayed for
I am thy God, I will still give thee aid.
I'll strengthen thee, help thee and cause thee
to stand. Upheld by my gracious,
omnipotent hand."

Keen

O God, our help in ages past,
our hope for years to come,
Our shelter from the stormy blast,
and our eternal home!

Isaac Watts

The Shepherd will not always replenish you in
the same way; His response to you will always
perfectly correspond to your present need.

Henry Blackaby

When you live a surrendered life, God is willing
and able to provide for your every need.

Corrie ten Boom

God provides for those who trust.

—

George Herbert

A Prayer

Lord, You have promised never to leave me or forsake me. You are always with me, protecting me and encouraging me. Whatever this day may bring, I thank You for Your love and for Your strength. Let me lean upon You, Father, this day and forever.

Amen

26

The Saving Heart of God

*For God so loved the world
that He gave His only begotten Son,
that whoever believes in Him
should not perish
but have everlasting life.*
John 3:16 NKJV

The heart of God is a saving heart. The familiar words of John 3:16 remind us of a profound truth: God loves each of us so much that He sent His Son to die for our sins.

Your Heavenly Father offers you the priceless gift of eternal life. How will you respond? Christ sacrificed His life on the cross so that you might be with Him throughout eternity. This gift, freely given from God's only begotten Son, is a priceless possession, a treasure beyond price, yet it is freely offered to you.

God is waiting patiently for each of us to accept the gift of eternal life. Let us claim Christ's gift today. Let us walk with the Savior; let us love Him; let us praise Him; and let us share His message of salvation with the world.

Grace comes from the heart of a gracious God
who wants to stun you and overwhelm you with
a gift you don't deserve—salvation, adoption,
a spiritual ability to use in kingdom service,
answered prayer, the church, His presence,
His wisdom, His guidance, His love.

Bill Hybels

God is glorified when people believe His gospel,
love His son, and accept His diagnosis of their
greatest need, which is forgiveness of sin.
You certainly benefit from God's provision
of salvation, but you exist for the glory of God.

John MacArthur

Before a man can be saved, he must feel
a consuming spiritual hunger.
Where a hungry heart is found,
we may be sure that God was there first.

A.W. Tozer

The eternal plan to reconcile man
with God and bridge the separation,
to save him from judgment for that sin,
to forgive him of all sins,
originated in the heart of God.

—

Anne Graham Lotz

A Prayer

*My salvation is in You, O Lord. My soul
finds rest in You through Your Son,
Jesus Christ. The gift of salvation brings
meaning to my life on earth because
I possess the assurance of eternal life
with You in heaven. I will praise You and
honor You, Father, today and forever.
Amen*

27

The Eternal Heart of God

Before the mountains were brought forth,
Or ever You had formed
the earth and the world,
Even from everlasting to everlasting,
You are God.
Psalm 90:2 NKJV

The heart of God is eternal and unchanging. Before God laid the foundations of our universe, He was a being of infinite power and love, and He will remain so throughout all eternity.

We humans are in a state of constant change. We are born, we grow, we mature, and we die. Along the way, we experience the inevitable joys and hardships of life. And we face the inevitable changes that are the result of our own mortality.

But God never changes. His love never ceases, His wisdom never fails, and His promises endure, unbroken, forever.

Place your trust in an eternal, unchanging God. Rest assured that His eternal heart will love you as much tomorrow as He does today and forever.

God is not affected by our mutability;
our changes do not alter him. When we are
restless, He remains serene and calm; when we
are low, selfish, mean, or dispirited, He is still
the unalterable I Am. The same yesterday, today,
and forever, in whom is no variableness, neither
shadow of turning. What God is in Himself,
not what we may chance to feel Him in this or
that moment to be, that is our hope.

Frederick William Robertson

Rejoice, that the immortal God is born,
so that mortal man may live in eternity.

Jan Hus

In God there is no was or will be, but a continuous
and unbroken is. In him history and prophecy
are one and the same.

A. W. Tozer

Christ is like a river that is continually flowing.
There are always fresh supplies of water coming
from the fountain-head, so that a man may live
by it and be supplied with water all his life.
So Christ is an ever-flowing fountain;
he is continually supplying his people,
and the fountain is not spent. They who live
upon Christ may have fresh supplies from him
for all eternity; they may have an increase of
blessedness that is new, and new still, and
which never will come to an end.

—

Jonathan Edwards

A Prayer
Dear Lord, I praise You that You are eternal.
There was never a time when You did not exist nor
will there be a time when You will not be. Thank
You that You will never change, and that You will
never stop loving me. And, while I am in this world,
I will pass through it with praise on my lips and
love in my heart for You.
Amen

28

The Attentive Heart of God

"For I know the thoughts that
I think toward you," says the LORD,
"thoughts of peace and not of evil,
to give you a future and a hope.
Then you will call upon Me
and go and pray to Me,
and I will listen to you."

Jeremiah 29:11, 12 NKJV

*G*od is not distant, and He is not disinterested. To the contrary, your Heavenly Father is very interested in everything about you. In fact, God knows precisely what you need and when you need it. But, He still wants to talk with you, and if you're a faithful believer, you should want to talk to Him too.

Jesus made it clear to His disciples that even though God knew their needs, they should pray always. And so should we. Genuine, heartfelt prayer changes things and it changes us. When we lift our hearts to our Father in heaven, we open ourselves to a never-ending source of divine wisdom and infinite love.

Do you have questions that you simply can't answer? Ask for the guidance of your Creator. Do you sincerely seek the gift of everlasting love and eternal life? Accept the grace of God's only begotten Son. Whatever your need, no matter how great or small, pray about it. Instead of waiting for mealtimes or bedtimes, follow the instruction of your Savior: pray always and never lose heart. And remember: God is not simply near; He is attentive to what is happening to you, and He wants to talk with you. Now!

Prayer is request. The essence of request, as distinct from compulsion, is that it may or may not be granted. And if an infinitely wise being listens to the requests of finite and foolish creatures, of course He will sometimes grant and sometimes refuse them.

C. S. Lewis

You can talk to God because God listens. Even if you stammer or stumble, even if what you have to say impresses no one, it impresses God, and he listens.

Max Lucado

When we pray, the first thing we should do is to see to it that we really get an audience with God, that we really get into His very presence. Before a word of petition is offered, we should have the definite consciousness that we are talking to God, and we should believe that He is listening.

R. A. Torrey

The key to a blessed life is to have
a listening heart that longs to know
what the Lord is saying.

—

Jim Cymbala

A Prayer

*Dear Lord, Your Holy Word commands me
to pray without ceasing. And You are always
listening. Let me take everything to You in
prayer. When I am discouraged, let me pray.
When I am lonely, let me take my sorrows to
You. When I grieve, let me take my tears to
You, Lord, in prayer. And when I am joyful,
let me offer up prayers of thanksgiving. In all
things great and small, at all times, whether
happy or sad, let me seek Your wisdom and
Your Grace...in prayer.*
Amen

29

The Renewing Heart of God

*Therefore we do not lose heart.
Even though our outward man
is perishing, yet the inward man
is being renewed day by day.*
2 Corinthians 4:16 NKJV

God intends that His children lead joyous lives filled with abundance and peace. But sometimes, abundance and peace seem very far away. It is then that we must turn to God for renewal, and when we do, He will restore us.

Are you tired or troubled? Turn your prayers toward the renewing heart of God. Are you weak or worried? Study God's Word and contemplate on its meaning for your life. Are you spiritually depleted? Call upon fellow Christians to lift you up, and call upon Christ to renew your faith and your strength. When you do, you'll discover that your Heavenly Father is, indeed, a God of renewal And you will discover that He is always willing to create a new sense of wonderment and joy in you.

Like a spring of pure water, God's peace
in our hearts brings cleansing and
refreshment to our minds and bodies.

Billy Graham

The same voice that brought Lazarus out of
the tomb raised us to newness of life.

C. H. Spurgeon

The amazing thing about Jesus is that
He doesn't just patch up our lives,
He gives us a brand new sheet,
a clean slate to start over, all new.

Gloria Gaither

Walking with God leads to receiving his intimate
counsel, and counseling leads to deep restoration.

John Eldredge

No matter how badly we have failed, we can always get up and begin again. Our God is the God of new beginnings.

—

Warren Wiersbe

A Prayer

Dear Lord, You can make all things new. I am a new creature in Christ Jesus, and when I fall short in my commitment, You can renew my effort and my enthusiasm. When I am weak or worried, restore my strength, Lord, for my own sake and for the sake of Your kingdom.
Amen

30

The Generous Heart of God

*Blessed be the God and
Father of our Lord Jesus Christ,
who has blessed us with every
spiritual blessing in
the heavenly places in Christ,*

Ephesians 1:3 NKJV

*G*od's heart overflows with generosity and mercy. And as believers in a loving God, we must imitate our Heavenly Father to the best of our abilities. Because God has been so incredibly generous with us, we, in turn must be generous with others.

Jesus has much to teach us about generosity. He teaches that the most esteemed men and women are not the self-congratulatory leaders of society but are, instead, the humblest of servants (Matthew 23:11, 12).

If you were being graded on generosity, how would you score? Would you earn "A's" in philanthropy and humility? Hopefully so. But if your grades could stand a little improvement, today is the perfect day to begin.

Today, you may feel the urge to hoard your blessings. Don't do it. Instead, give generously to your neighbors, and do so without fanfare. Find a need and fill it...humbly. Lend a helping hand and share a word of kindness...anonymously. This is God's way.

Giving with glad and generous hearts has a way of
routing out the tough old miser within us.
Even the poor need to know that they can give.
Just the very act of letting go of money, or some
other treasure, does something within us.
It destroys the demon greed.

Richard J. Foster

In Jesus, the service of God and the service of
the least of the brethren were one.

Dietrich Bonhoeffer

Christianity, in its purest form, is nothing more
than seeing Jesus. Christian service, in its purest
form, is nothing more than imitating him who
we see. To see his Majesty and to imitate him:
that is the sum of Christianity.

Max Lucado

All the blessings we enjoy are Divine deposits,
committed to our trust on this condition,
that they should be dispensed for
the benefit of our neighbors.

John Calvin

Following Jesus means living as obedient
servants of his heavenly Father
and ministering—even suffering—
for the sake of others.

—

Stanley Grenz

A Prayer

*Dear Lord, in weak moments, I want to hoard
all my blessings to enjoy by myself.
But Your commandment, Lord, is that
I become a humble servant sharing with
those who need my encouragement, my help,
and my love. Instill in me the same generous
spirit that fills Your heart. Make me willing to
give so that my life may bring praise
and honor to You.
Amen*

31

The Transforming Heart of God

Therefore, if anyone is in Christ,
he is a new creation;
old things have passed away;
behold,
all things have become new.
2 Corinthians 5:17 NKJV

For many people, change is to be avoided at all costs. But the Bible makes it clear that God's ultimate goal for you and me is to change us. When we accept Christ into our hearts and genuinely invite Him to reign over our lives, we become different people—and this change is forever.

When we welcome Jesus into our hearts, an old life ends and a new life begins. God transforms our lives and gives us a completely new view of the world.

Let us then live out that transformed life. Each morning offers a fresh opportunity to invite Christ, yet once again, to rule over our hearts and our days. Each new day presents yet another opportunity to take up His cross and follow in His footsteps. Today, let us rejoice in the new life that is ours through Christ, and let us follow Him, step by step, on the path that He first walked.

There is no situation so chaotic that God cannot
from that situation create something that
is surpassingly good. He did it at the creation.
He did it at the cross. He is doing it today.

Handley Moule

There is nothing anybody else can do that
can stop God from using us.
We can turn everything into a testimony.

Corrie ten Boom

If the world controls your thinking, you are
a conformer; if God controls your thinking,
you are a transformer.

Warren Wiersbe

A person who really cares about his or her
neighbor, a person who genuinely loves others,
is a person who bears witness to the truth.

Anne Graham Lotz

The adventure of new life in Christ begins when the comfortable patterns of the old life are left behind.

—

David Roher

A Prayer

Dear Lord, the life that I live and the words that I speak bear testimony to my transformed life. Make me a faithful servant of Your Son, Jesus. Let my testimony be worthy of You: Let my words be sure and true, Lord, and let my actions point others to You.

Amen

Thoughts & Reflections

_____

_____

_____

_____

_____

_____

_____

_____

_____

_____

_____

_____

_____

_____

_____

_____

_____

_____

_____

Thoughts & Reflections

_____

_____

_____

_____

_____

_____

_____

_____

_____

_____

_____

_____

_____

_____

_____

_____

_____

_____

Thoughts & Reflections

Thoughts & Reflections

_____

_____

_____

_____

_____

_____

_____

_____

_____

_____

_____

_____

_____

_____

_____

_____

_____

Thoughts & Reflections

Thoughts & Reflections

_____

_____

_____

_____

_____

_____

_____

_____

_____

_____

_____

_____

_____

_____

_____

_____